ANDREW VACHSS

Another Chance To Get It Right

a children's book for adults

A portion of this publication originally appeared in
PARADE MAGAZINE June 16, 1991.

Published by
Dark Horse Comics, Inc., 10956 SE Main, Milwaukie, OR 97222.

Second trade paperback edition: March 1995
ISBN: 1-56971-115-1

Printed in Canada

DARK • HORSE • BOOKS

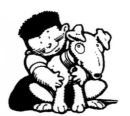

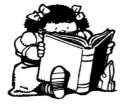

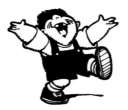

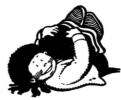

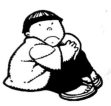

THIS BOOK BELONGS TO

A *bright fall day* at the Bronx Zoo. I was standing outside the bear pit, waiting. The pit was full: black bears, Kodiaks, Grizzlies, even a pair of tiny Japanese sun bears. Cavorting in the sunlight, diving into the water, mock-wrestling for the sheer joy of it. Early in the day, peaceful and quiet.

A flock of children descended on me. Hard to tell their ages, maybe six, eight years old? All dressed in school uniforms, but no two alike. Their teacher assembled them at the rail to the pit, patient with their eagerness, watchful against adventurous spirits wandering too close to the bears.

The children watched the bears — some solemn, some animated. One little girl waved gaily. A little boy shouted something. The bears ignored them all, being themselves.

I was there on business. Private business. So I moved along the catwalk to the next pit. A solitary polar bear stood atop a barren peak of rock, her white pelt blending against the ice. She watched the newcomer, self-contained and uncaring. A tiny sound from one of the caves. A fluffy white cub emerged, called to its mother. The bear's gaze turned malevolent, warning me to stay away. She charged down the slope to her cub, nudged him toward the icy water with her snout.

They swam together. Then she pushed him to the edge of the water, one massive paw lifting him to land. She drew the cub to her, licking him dry, icy eyes pinning me with a deadly warning.

"Is she guarding the baby?" A child's voice at my elbow. A little girl, detached from the school group.

"Yeah," I told her, wondering how she knew. An oriental child, her face was tranquil with wisdom. A white boy stood at her shoulder, a black girl next to him.

"My mother does that," she told me.

"Mine don't," the white boy said.

I lit a cigarette. A blonde girl tugged at my sleeve, pointing at the No Smoking sign. A handsome latino boy sneered at her naivete. I dropped the cigarette to the concrete, ground it out under my shoe. Looked over my shoulder, wondering when their teacher would come and collect them.

"Are they dangerous?" a little girl asked.

"Sure," I said.

"I'm not afraid," a boy proclaimed.

"I'd like to pat the baby," said another.

Maybe you will, someday, I thought, glancing at my watch.

"How come she's not with the other bears?" a boy asked.

"Because she has a baby. If the other bears came near her baby, she'd hurt them."

"Isn't she lonely?"

"She has her baby, stupid!" a little girl answered for me.

"So what?" another sneered.

I listened to them squabble, so distinct and unique in their matching uniforms. A rainbow of colors, a depthless vat of potential.

They could be ... get to be ... become ... anything.

A tug at my sleeve. "Mister, do you have any kids?"

I looked at the bear. "I don't know," I told the child.

As I walked away, I heard her ask the teacher what the strange man meant.

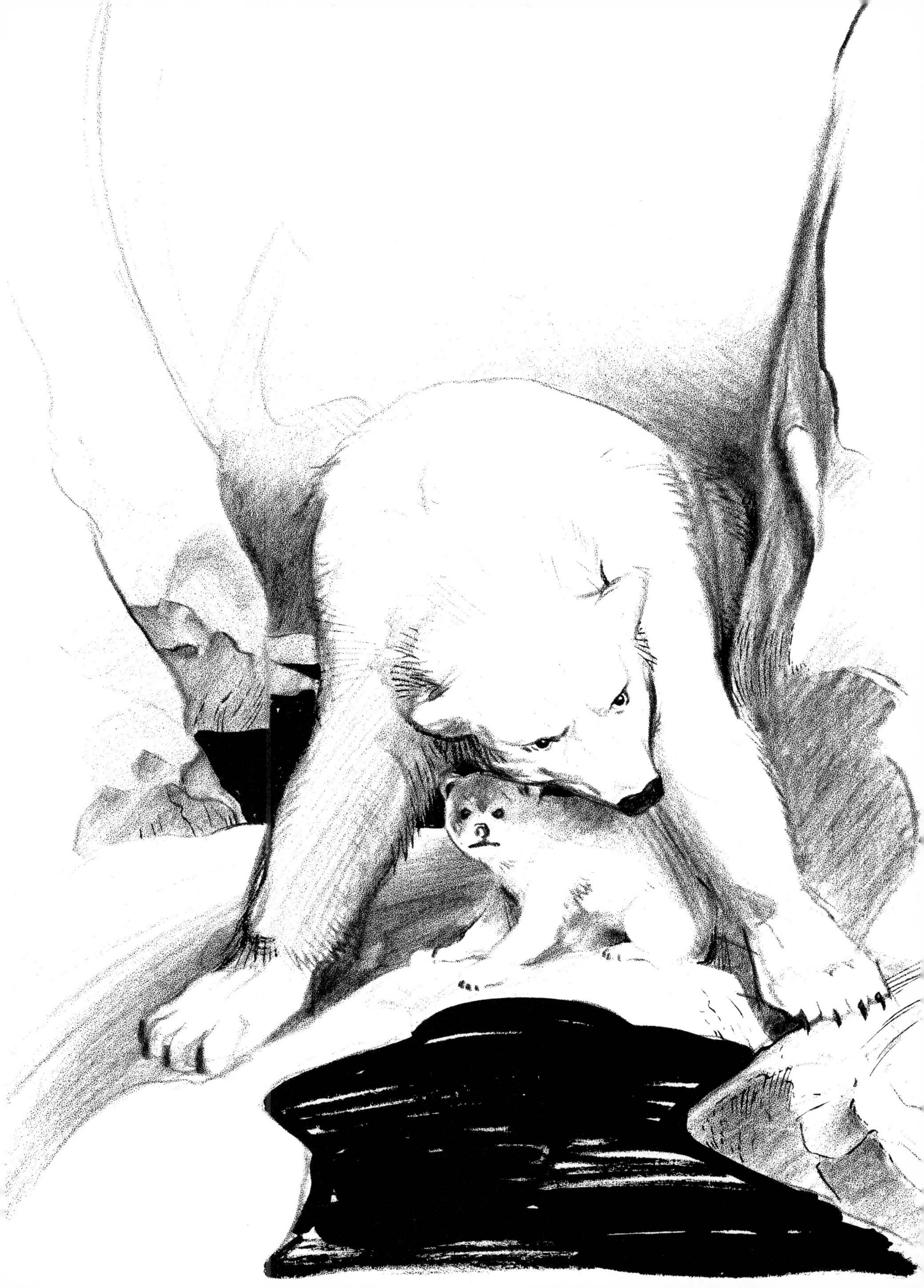

What is the difference between an elephant and an alligator?" the old man asked me. It wasn't a question, it was the way he taught. The way his ancestors have taught since the beginning of his tribe.

"One's a mammal, one's a reptile. One lives on land and visits water, one lives in water and visits land. One is a flesh-eater, the other a vegetarian. Neither have natural enemies."

"But both are hunted, yes?"

"Yes, I see. The elephants for their ivory, the alligators for their hides. They have the same enemy — man."

"You do not see. I asked you the difference, not the similarity."

"I told you many differences."

"Yet you missed the essential one. The difference that separates them forever."

"Is this a riddle?"

"Not a riddle, not a mystery. A truth you can learn ... if you listen."

"I'm listening."

"The baby alligator comes out of the egg a perfectly-formed predator. It will not grow, it will only get larger, do you see? It learns nothing. From the moment of its birth, it fights to survive. If it succeeds, if it reaches its full size, it hunts. At birth, it is six inches long. In adulthood, perhaps six feet. The difference

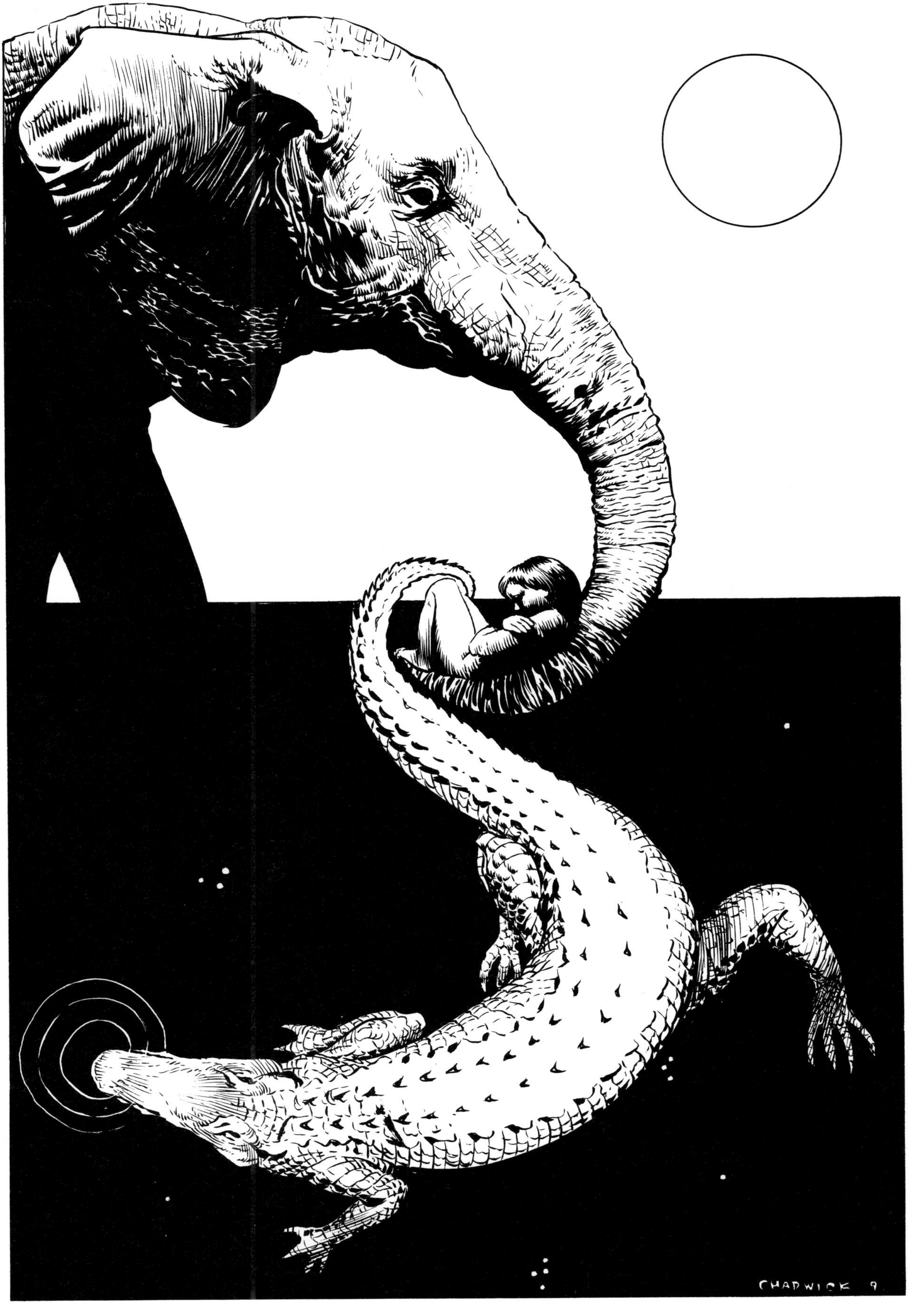
CHADWICK 9

can be measured. As a predator, it increases in power, in skill. But no matter what its fate, it will always be what it was born to be."

"I understand."

"Do you? Your work is with children. To work with children, you must know the child. The baby elephant cannot survive on its own. It needs nurturing, it needs protection. Without love, it dies. Depending on how it is raised, the baby elephant grows to be a work animal, a circus performer, a peaceful beast content to live in harmony with the herd, its family. But some elephants grow up to be rogues, dangerous to man. Depending on how they are raised, that is the key. You see the difference now?"

"Yes."

"And so, ask yourself, are the children of men alligators, doomed to be what they will be from the moment of their birth ... or are they elephants, fated to be nothing specific ... and capable of anything?"

*C*hildren dance. First with light and shadow, sound and smell. Born in liquid blindness, they reach out from the most elemental of needs.

The heart is the last to go searching.

Some touch silk, some fire.

Some master their environments and seek others.

Some are swallowed, cut off before full bloom.

And some bloom deadly nightshade.

On the upper tier of a maximum-security youth prison, I watched a gang of larger, older inmates approach a slightly-built boy. They surrounded him, pressing him back against the cold green cinderblock wall, making their ugly intentions clear. The smaller boy, a veteran of orphanages and detention homes, watched them warily, eyes unblinking as he memorized their faces.

Finally, he smiled. "You all have to sleep sometime," he said, his voice a chilly whisper.

They left him alone after that.

Children absorb, imitate, innovate. Their play is preparation: the mannered posturing of a formal tea dance, the survival-driven cooperation of the wolf pack.

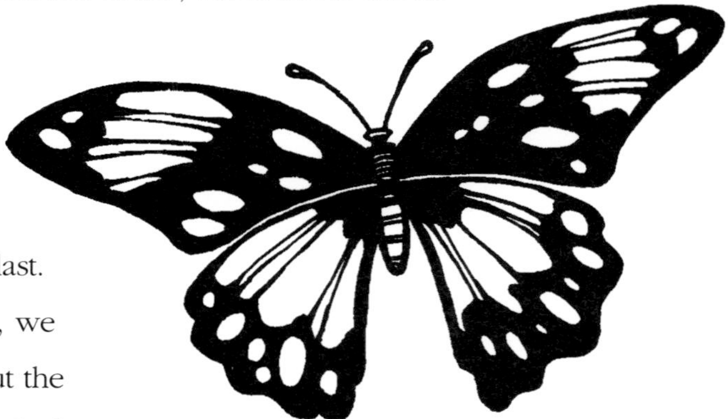

All children have half-lives. A life as a child, and a life beyond. The first compels the last.

Children are beauty, we are fond of saying. But without the bedrock that is their birthright, the beauty is short-lived. Even the loveliest butterfly must eventually land. Or die.

All butterflies land. They land in the rain forest; they land in the city canyons. Some alight gently, adding their essence to the continual process of the earth's renewal. Others fall to earth, and become one with it. We can quantify a child's needs, we can make out checklists with great care. But even the World Health Organization doesn't list *love* as a nutrient. And the psychiatric manuals don't list *evil* as a diagnosis.

We call birth a miracle. What greater word fits adoption?

Childhood is full of promise. For some, the promise is a whore's kiss. And some are born without the price.

As the twig is bent, so grows the tree. Saplings reach toward the sun. But there are many suns in a child's sky.

Some nourish. And some sear.

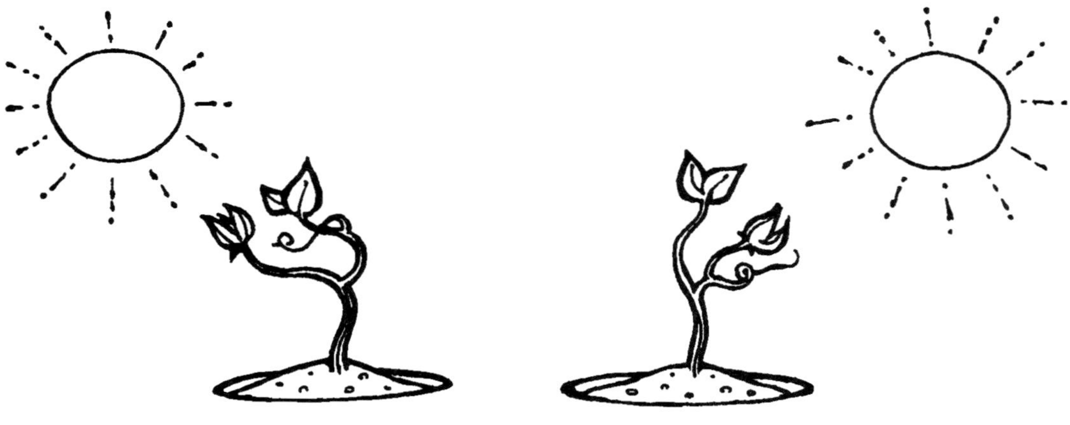

I know a man so hard that predators step aside when he walks. A violence-artist, he has used his hands to make a living since childhood, from professional prize-fighting to underworld debt collection. Raised in orphanages and reform schools, educated in prison, he plays the few cards dealt to him with great viciousness. His eyes are ball bearings, his smile a snarl. His very presence suggests menace.

In his world, softness is cancer.

He was visiting me one day to sort out a problem he was having with his past. The conversation became intense as his options narrowed. His daughter, a blossoming child of three, resplendent in a new pair of overalls, played noisily on the floor of my office. Finally, bored with the adult conversation, she demanded attention, pulling at her father's sleeve, refusing to be ignored. She became louder and louder, drowning out any attempt to communicate. The hard man turned to her, displayed a scarred fist that looked like a lump of old leather, and told her if she didn't shut up immediately, he'd knock her head off her body.

The little girl's body shook with delighted laughter at such a ridiculous statement.

The human animal is never truly self-sufficient. Babies are the personification of need. Children are needy. And the need to give, to love is the transfusion that mutates the feral savagery into which we all are born.

Empathy. To feel the pain of another as our own.

Hardest to learn, the most valuable of all we are allowed to feel.

Relationships are formalized, with family hierarchy as rigid and immutable as history. And as ephemeral as flower petals arranged by a whimsical breeze, living for a micro-second. Relationships are independent organisms, reacting to stimulus as a whole and as parts of that whole. They are subsumed into work, play, pursuit.

A child watching her mother prepare tribal food learns more than the skills she will strive so hard to emulate. The boy permitted to join the hunt for the first time hunts more than food.

A child is: awestruck at a butterfly emerging from a cocoon. Struck dumb with terror at a soldier's footsteps. Comforted by a kitten's trusting warmth. An invisible spider's web too complex to chart, the strands of relationships are re-woven throughout life. Some bond with safety until the launch. Some bind, strangling.

They are, and they will be.

Divided by an economic chasm, yet driven by the same primacy, one mother picks through rags in a bombed-out ruin while another lovingly arranges a black and white mobile over her baby's crib. A father pushes his body past tolerance, working days, laboring nights. Another opens a trust fund, planning a glowing future for a child not yet born.

On the other side of the world, and a few blocks away, evil does its work. Children are sold by families too poor to feed them. And forced to dance in the White Light District of kiddie pornography.

Humanity's worst crime exists in no statute book: What would the lawmaker's call the theft of childhood?

Children are us before we are. And we are indelibly marked by how we mark them.

Everyone admires a chubby baby. Is that because we know babies are only fat in peacetime?

> I saw an infant lying against a tree deep inside a war-torn jungle, too weak to cry. A woman ran past me, covered only with a strip of cloth, a tiny knife in her hand. She stopped, scooped the baby into one arm, and kept running. A blood-bonded adoption, driven by an instinct no war could kill.

A man beams with pride, proclaiming his gratitude to the gods that his daughter resembles only her beautiful mother.

Another basks in the counter-genetic horror of incest.

Biology does not make a man a father — nor a woman a mother.

We are what we *do*.

There is learning in play, play in learning.

Terror in fear, heroism in its mastery.

The universals? Some say biology dictates that all children are appealing — they contribute so little and take so much, how else would they survive? Yet ... what they contribute is a gestalt ... more than the combination of love and joy and need.

In the world's darkness, the fierce glow of a baby's eyes is a goad to great sacrifice for adoring parents. And in some darker corners, a beacon for rats.

Even as they explore, children seek permanency. Foundation. Bedrock. Safety. Permanency is sought in the exploration of limits. A child thrust into a pitch-black room reaches out to find the walls. Too late we learn to fear the consequences of a child who finds all he needs ... and all he trusts ...within himself.

Stability is sought by testing, by play, in relationships, and by responses ... by reassurances from a world that grows ever less anonymous as children merge and become one with it.

But relationships themselves are not permanent. As patternless as desert sands, subject to stronger forces. And, yet, always there. There can be permanency in a nomadic tribe whose daily existence is circumscribed by the search for food and shelter. And drifting on the streets of the richest cities in the world.

Children test. They test limits even as their growth makes mountains of the past into plateaus from which they spring to new heights. They test the tensile strength of their cribs — the emotional strength of their parents. They test friendships, and, in the process, themselves.

This testing is natural, organic, dictated into the genetic coding of every species. Parenting is a balance: the baby's first steps must be monitored, guarded against mishap. But always encouraged, so that someday the child walks free. To continue the cycle.

The most delicate balance, on the highest wire. And some must do this work without a safety net.

The very existence of children tests us all. Their new birth tests us anew. They test our pretty words and pat phrases. Hypocrisy cannot survive a child's gaze ... that stare so simultaneously guileless and relentless.

We have laws that prohibit child labor in the same countries in which children are sold as chattel.

Children are worshipped in some places, executed in others.

Oh yes: the devil can quote the scriptures.

"In the best interests of the child ... "

"For their own good ... "

Watch a child with a puppy. See the untarnished pure love flow between them as an electric current. The current remains through the years, but its poles alter according to species. The child always loves, but loves other things as growth impacts on his expanding world. The puppy grows too, but with an animal's linear truth. Step into the current flowing between them and feel the shock.

Watch, and learn why slaves were never allowed to own dogs.

• • • • •

In nature, nothing blooms in a vacuum.

But adults arbitrarily assign importance to factors nature would dismiss. We exalt our fears and prejudices with nice words that end in "ism." Soon the territoriality of the pack is technologically expanded. Then our historians and rhetoricians enter an unholy race to achieve the ultimate in justificatory language.

Justifying racism, hunger, deprivation. War.

All over this globe, our tribes war.

Never fighting our common enemy, tribalism.

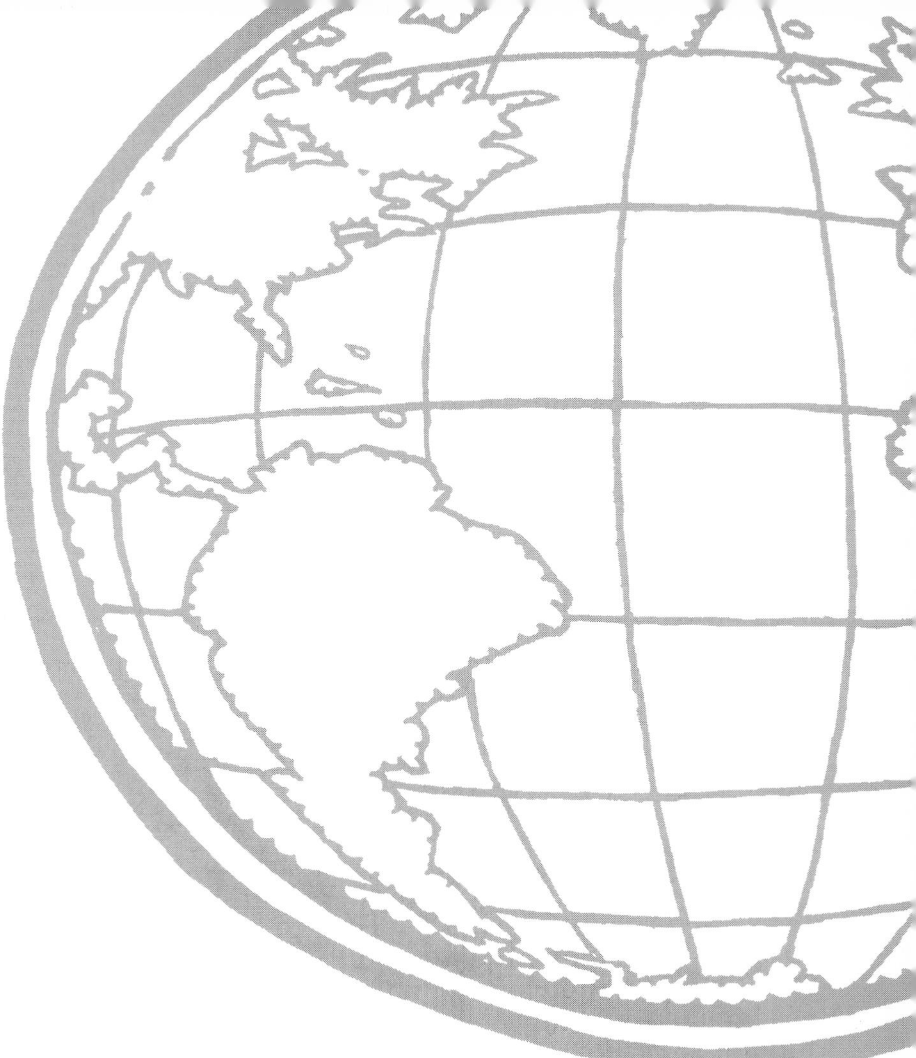

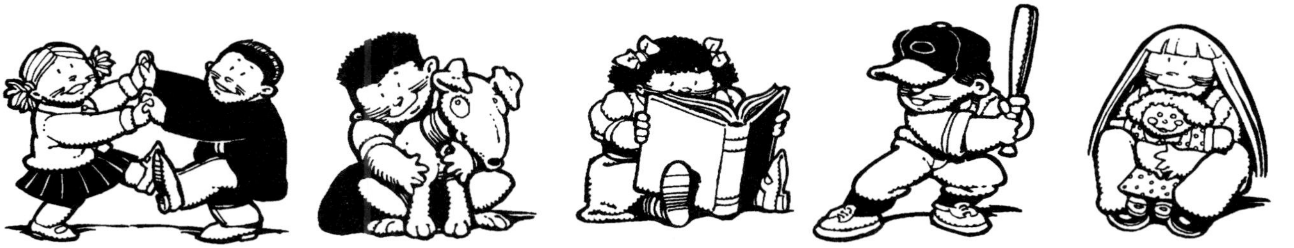

Two decades ago, I was on the perimeter of a dirt-track landing strip in Africa. Warplanes dominated the night, unseen menace. Death rained from the air, bombs and tracers. Death reigned on the ground too, where food was a myth. The humans in the air called the land Nigeria. Their brothers and sisters on the ground called it Biafra. As in all history, vocabulary disputes are settled by violence.

The ground exploded. Some ran, adrenalin dictating what malnutrition had robbed. Some froze. Fear running, fear frozen.

A child clutched at my jacket. I couldn't tell his age. His body was a starving ten year old's. His face was ancient. "Why do you run?" he asked. "The bombs cannot see you."

He pointed at the sights and sounds shaping the night. "If you run, the bombs hit you. If you stay, the bombs hit you. Better to stay."

I sat down, feeling the beyond-fear calm of a person abandoned to forces past comprehension. The boy sat next to me. "Have you got a cigarette?" he asked.

I often wonder ... if he survived.

And if he did, what he is, now.

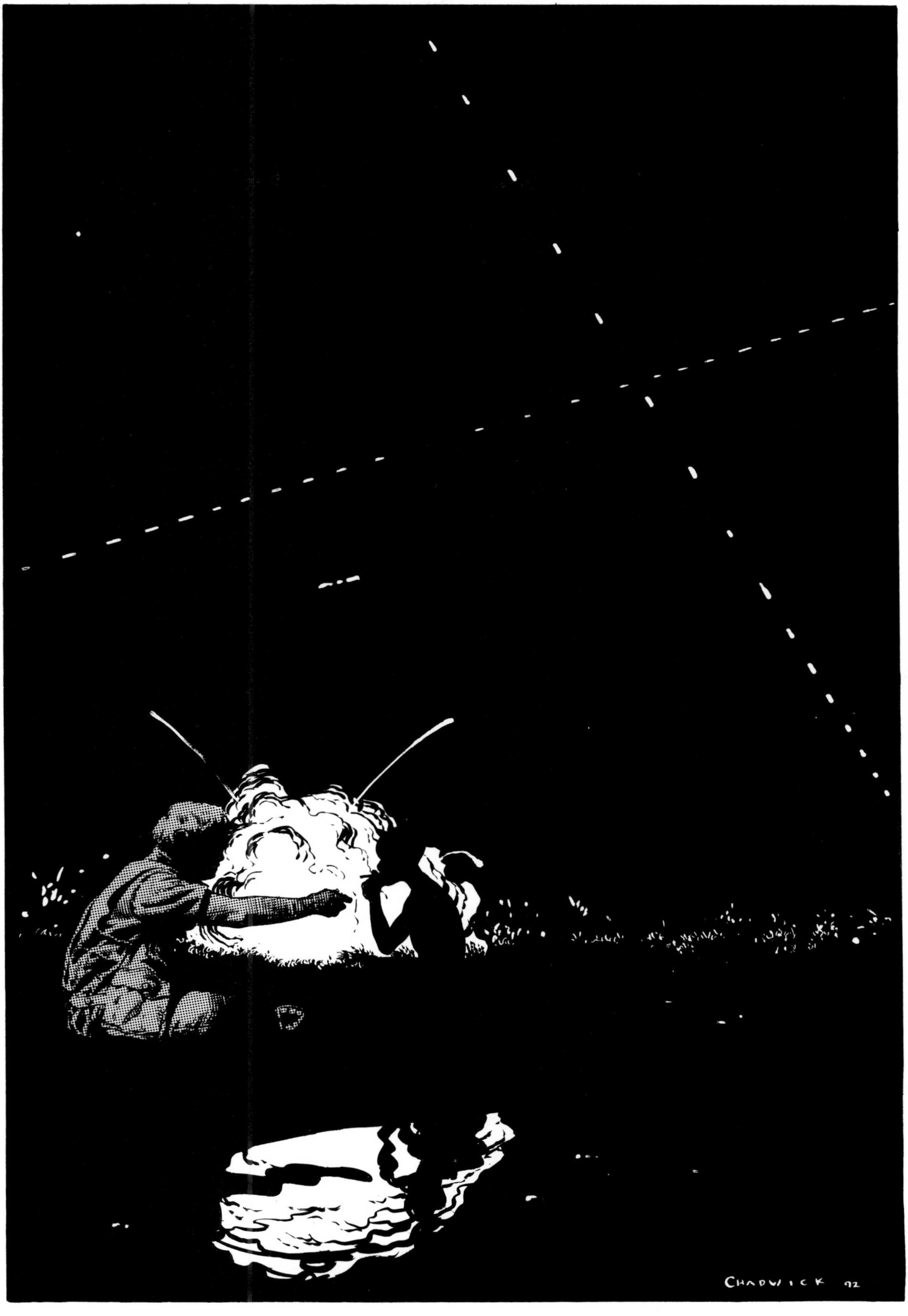
CHADWICK 92

*S*urvival-driven need has its own volumetric efficiency. The Venturi principle dominates: when space is restricted, speed increases. Hunger, poverty, pain ... all increase thrust.

And some fall off the unbanked speedway.

• • • • •

Are the child's eyes wide with wonder? Or with fear?

None among us exclusively owns the Rosetta Stone. What we see is our truth, not the child's.

What we see reveals us. And what we do with what we see distinguishes us.

Throughout the world, there are many climates. But, within them, always there is weather.

Our rituals are not celebrations *for* children, but *of* them. Baptism, bar mitzvah, birthdays. We seek to mark the life-passages indelibly, as if to affirm our hopes. Such celebrations are planned with military precision, love and pride commingling. Celebration as display.

But children's own celebrations are spontaneous eruptions. Unplanned, explosive, short-lived. Treasures dimly recalled as adults, never to be as fully and viscerally unearthed again.

Children learn, and they teach. The best teachers are those who refuse to stop learning.

Children learn by imitation. Some imitate their oppressors, and we call them monsters.

A child meets a stranger, tilts her face up, expecting a kiss. Another's eyes are wary. Asking, "Are you going to hurt me too?"

For a child, there is no sequence, there is only merger. It all happens together.

Only the adults know what to call it.

Only a child can feel it.

• • • • •

We are tested, and sometimes we fail. The maltreated child cries "I hurt." Unheard or unheeded, that cry becomes prophecy.

"Do unto others" becomes a battle cry.

When rituals fail, interpretation becomes experiential, as varied as each child is unique. The child seeks the concepts, and is confronted by the symbols. But the symbols are clouded by the facile ease with which the adult world re-interprets words hardened in the crucible of greed. Explain "situational ethics" to a child. If you can.

And so the child says: "I can make a life — I am a man." And the world has more children.

And the child says: "I can take a life — I am a man." And the world has less.

If you could listen to a child's soul ... you might hear the lush blendings of a symphony ... or a harsh, cold metronome: tick, tick, tick ...

A bomb, awaiting its time.

• • • • •

Children are all the same. Genetic variations immaterial. Cultural variations but flowers in the earth's bouquet.

Children transcend. Born to war, they become healers. Born to privilege, they become warriors.

Within us all is that root of recognition. When we were all one.

One child.

Oh, that we could learn to recognize one another in the darkness.

On the roof of a tenement building, two small boys have fashioned a spaceship from a packing crate. It was laborious work, salvaging bits and pieces for their project from the city streets, working from a blueprint that lived only in their heads. The original configuration followed the shape of the packing crate, forcing one boy to sit behind the other. For some reason, their ship would not soar no matter which of them took the controls. Much weighty discussion followed. More tearing apart and pounding together. Finally, there was room for the boys to sit side-by-side. They visited strange planets together and had many adventures.

The older sister of one of the boys came to the roof one day to take in the washing. Hearing excited voices, she looked inside. Discovered, the two pals carefully and patiently explained that their ship was magic. A special ship, one that could truly fly. The older sister was wise beyond her years, and did not ask to go along on their trips.

Time passed, and the spaceship valiantly withstood rain and wind, always ready for a mission. The family of one of the boys moved to another neighborhood. Not so far away, maybe, but too far for the little ones to travel on their own. The older sister was a good and loving child herself, but a teenager absorbed in the mysteries of adolescence. The roof was her private place too, a place to be alone with her dreams. She climbed the stairs to the outside air a few weeks later, ostensibly to bring down the wash. Busy with her work and with her dreams, it was a while before she noticed her precious little brother standing by her side, looking mournfully at the ship.

"Why don't you take a ride?" she asked.

The little boy looked up at her, truth shining from his eyes. "Bobby is gone, sis," he said. "Our ship won't fly anymore."

The young girl was saving the money she earned from babysitting on Saturday afternoons — her only free time. She was saving for a special sweater that she had coveted for what seemed like forever. The next Saturday, she cancelled her babysitting job and took her little brother on a long bus ride. When they returned, her brother's pal was with them.

The spaceship never soared so beautifully as on that day.

*T*he *riverfront* had only one industry — human pleasure. Gambling dens, whore houses, gin mills. Anything could be had for a price — only life was cheap.

I had been looking for a man for some weeks. A professional gambler. He had been named as a sexual contact by a prostitute found to be infected with syphilis. My job was to find him, determine if he too was infected. And, if so, get a list of his partners. And find them.

Syphilis is a virulent, deadly disease — sexually transmitted. Easily treated, if you get there in time. And thus, theoretically, susceptible to eradication. John infects Mary, Mary infects Bill, Bill infects Susan. Or Sam. All chains. We could never find the root, so our task was to break the links.

The disease is hemopathic. It takes many forms, the original symptoms fading quickly, giving the false illusion of cure. But it lurks, incubating. And when it flowers, its ravages are permanent.

The natives call it Bad Blood.

I began in Chicago, learning the interviewing and investigation techniques. We had a sense of mission — there was a reason for what we did. But I'd been out a long time: penthouses to migrant labor camps, schoolyards to prisons. I was losing sight of the mission

concentrating on individual tasks. You use your eyes and your ears. Persuading, cajoling, pressuring.

Watching

and waiting.

Mother and fetus share a common blood supply. So a baby may be born with congenital syphilis.

When I started this work, I thought that was the only way a baby could be infected — the worst thing that could happen to a child.

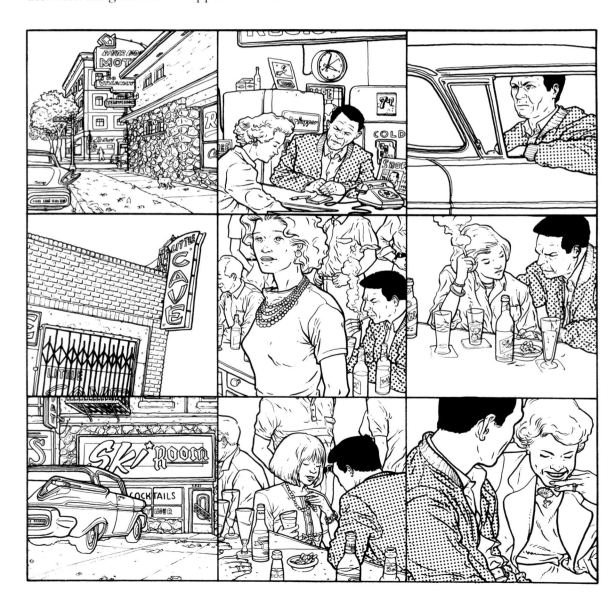

I was wrong.

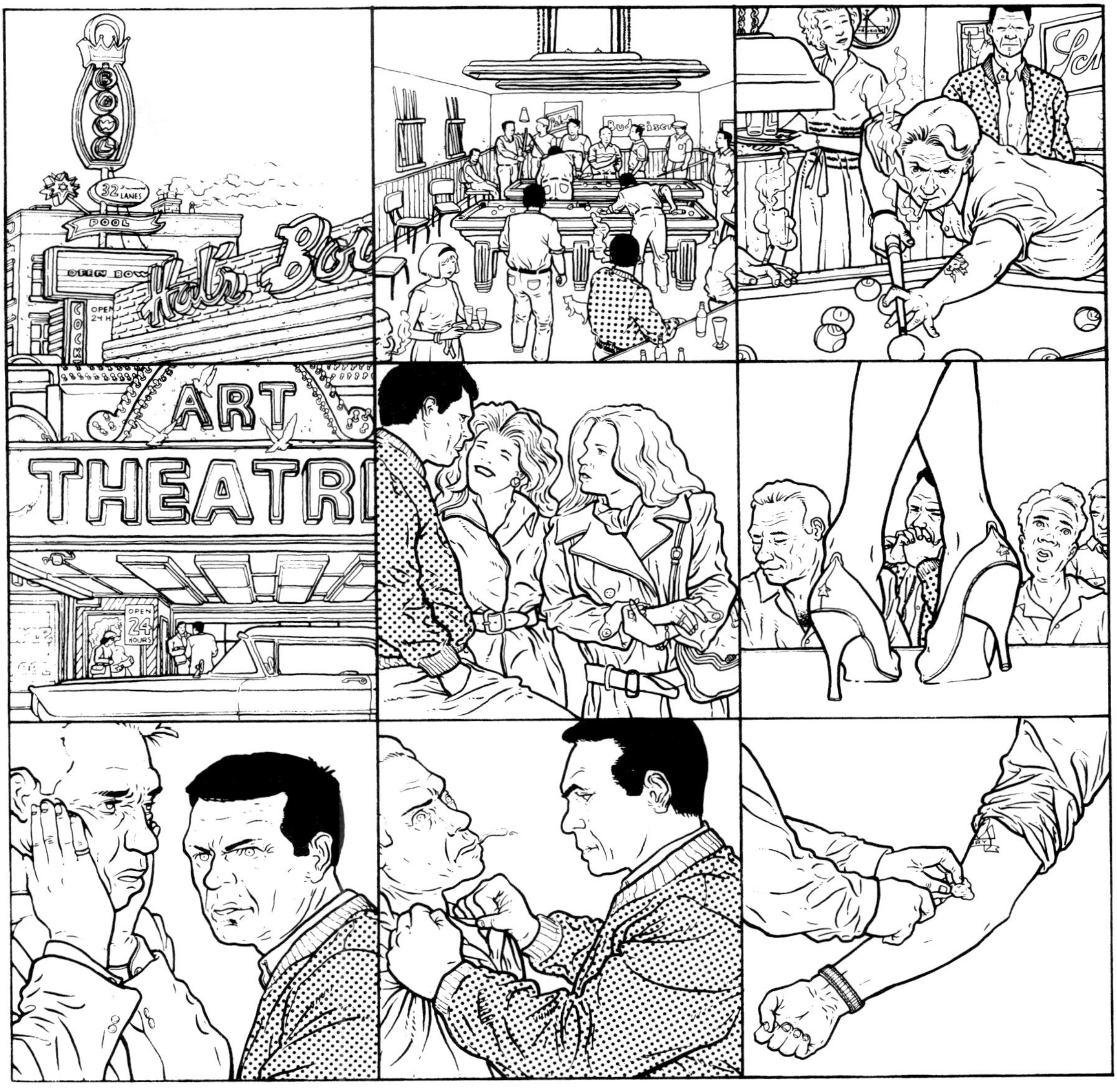

32 LANES
POOL
ART
OPEN 24 HOURS

A seamless job,

it seemed.

Each target produced others,

multiplying.

Swimming toward a horizon,

fighting an

unwinnable

war.

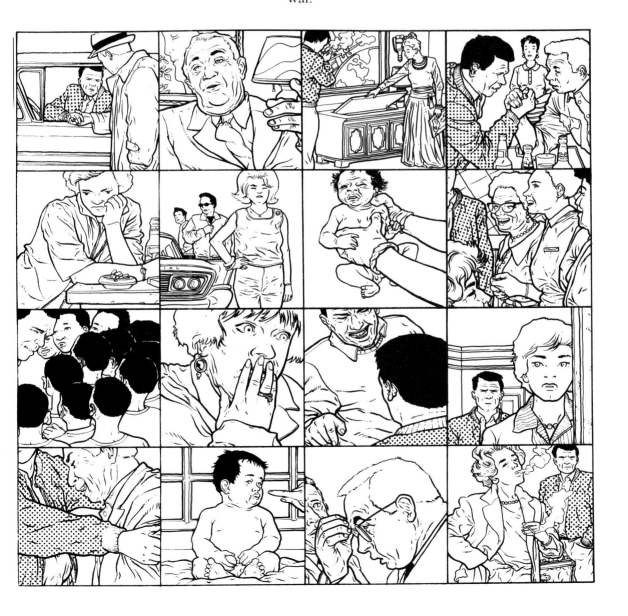

I stepped out the back door of a night club into a humid summer night. A little past midnight. I'd invested hours in the club, all for nothing. Just the trace of a lead ... my man had been spotted in a joint on the other side of the river, in West Virginia. It wasn't much to go on — tomorrow would be soon enough to try.

I turned down the alley heading for the street where I'd left my car. The alley was washed in garish neon, music and loud voices came through the thin walls of the surrounding buildings. I lit a last cigarette, feeling more tired than a day's work should make a man.

A tow-headed little boy was standing before some discarded barrels, rigid at attention, watching something intently. A ragged, wild little child, maybe six years old. Where was his mother? Was he hunting for food? Lost?

I deliberately scraped a boot on the pavement, letting him know he wasn't alone.

He ignored me.

I squatted down next to him, said "Hello" softly so as not to frighten him. He held a grubby finger to his lips, commanding quiet. I watched him for a minute, impressed by his absorption, his total concentration. I followed his eyes, trying to see what he saw.

It took another couple of minutes. A pair of yellow eyes gleamed in the dark. Cat's eyes, cold and feral. Was the boy so fascinated by an alley cat?

"Where's your mother?" I whispered to him.

"In there," he said, indicating the night club. His eyes never left the cat.

What was the big deal?

I smoked another cigarette, slowly. Watching the boy watch the cat, my eyes adjusting to the night. I heard a faint mewing, saw a stirring in the inky blackness. And I saw why the cat hadn't simply run off. Her body almost covered a brood of tiny kittens.

"She's guarding them," the little boy said, his voice vibrating with the wonder of such a thing.

I awkwardly patted the boy on the shoulder. Got in my car and started the engine, thinking it through.

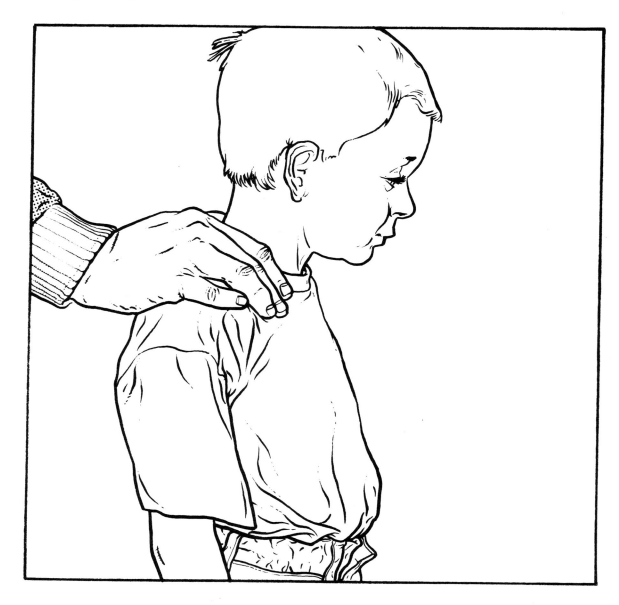

Then I headed for the bridge to West Virginia.

For the first slice of his life, it was only the boy and his mother. The father was overseas, protecting his wife and child on the battlefields of Europe. He wrote to his son every chance he got, explaining things in advance against the chance that he would never have the opportunity to do so in person. His father before him had given his life for his country in World War I — he knew the odds.

The boy's mother read to him constantly, his earliest education. But she never read her husband's letters — they were private, between a man and his son.

To this day, only the boy has read them. Many times.

His father deserved the medals they bestowed on him, and more.

He was his mother's medal.

By the time the father returned to his family, his dreams of a professional football career had been left in Europe. And his growing family made completing his college education impossible. He settled down to work toward his remaining goal — a better life for his children than his had been.

The boy's mother loved roses. Someday, she said, she would grow some of her own. The boy never knew all his parents dreams when he was a child.

Both parents worked hard, uncomplaining, their eyes on a horizon only their children might someday reach. After some years,

they bought a tiny tract house outside the city. In a better place for their children, they thought. This added hours to the father's work day. He never complained.

The children were saddened at leaving their friends, but rebounded with the resiliency of childhood. If their mother felt sorrow, she never showed it.

The new house was surrounded by a small patch of mean, shallow dirt. The yard. To city-born children, a vast meadow. The mother planted her rose bushes, and the red flowers bloomed despite everything.

That first summer, the neighborhood suffered an attack of voracious Japanese beetles. No one knew where they came from, those bronze-colored little monsters. But when it was discovered that they feasted on rose bushes, the boy believed they came from Hell itself. His mother sprayed insecticide diligently, to no avail. They came in waves, unstoppable. The boy would sit for hours, carefully plucking the beetles off the bushes, trying to save his mother's roses.

He failed.

His mother said someday the beetles would go away. She could always plant again.

To save his mother's treasures, the boy used the gift she gave him. Reading. He haunted the local library until he found his answer. Japanese beetles had one natural enemy, the Praying Mantis. Fearsome insects with huge front claws, capable of holding their prey until it was devoured. The nature book he consulted showed a picture of their egg sacs. They looked like a dull, fibrous mass, about the size of a golf ball. The color of dirt.

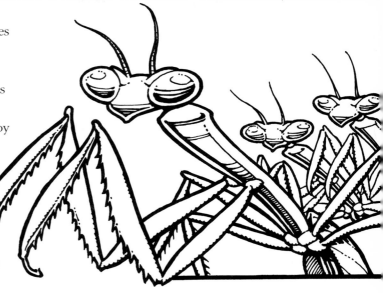

The boy scoured the vacant lots, collecting hundreds of the egg sacs, plotting. Each sac was carefully placed in a glass jar, left on the window sill to hatch.

And hatch they did. Hundreds, maybe thousands of tiny monsters burst forth from each one. He poured jar after jar of the hatchlings onto the rose bushes. Until they reached full growth, they were easy prey for birds and other predators. But the boy so inundated the bushes that they were blanketed with life, growing faster than the birds could feed.

The survivors were as single-minded in their consumption of Japanese beetles as the beetles had been of the roses. It was no contest, but the boy showed no mercy. Soon, the entire neighborhood was infested with Praying Mantis armies, the beasts growing to several inches as they fed so readily. They disposed of every Japanese beetle in the area, and immediately sought other prey. Sometimes, they swarmed so thick you couldn't see the vegetation.

The neighbors complained. The cure was worse than the disease, they said.

The boy's mother kissed him, telling him it was a wonderful thing he did, but to be careful not to go too far with things in life.

Advice he has not heeded since.

The boy and one of his younger brothers went back to their old neighborhood a couple of years ago. It was a blinding-bright summer day. They cruised the streets, remarking on the sites of some of the younger brother's more legendary battles with local bullies he had vanquished. Remembering how the boy had taught his little brother to ride a bike by mounting him on top of a hill and blithely pushing him off. The little tract houses had been transformed with time and a burgeoning real estate market. Second stories had been constructed, garages stood proudly. Some were beautifully landscaped.

They found their old house. It didn't look at all the same, but a rose bush bloomed in the front yard. And there wasn't a Japanese beetle in sight.

*J*ust as I was leaving childhood for adolescence, our family relocated. I met another boy the day we moved in, and he instantly became my best friend — the kind of weighty, high-speed decision only children can make. We built forts in the woods, piloted a canoe we made from a cut-down oil drum through the swampy canals surrounding an abandoned brickworks, conducted our scientific experiments, shared secrets. He was going to be a marine biologist — I was going to be something important.

My father was an abused child. Not by his father, who died when he was a boy. Abused by his mother's new husband. The abuse stopped when my father got his growth. After standing up to a male (I will not call him a man) who communicated with a razor strop, busting through a clot of rival football players seemed easy enough. My father never grew tall, he grew broad. A blocky, powerful man with a thick neck, a barrel chest, and hands that could crush. I knew the latter only from watching, never through experience. Defying the myth that all abused children grow up to be abusing parents, my father was a bear in the streets and a gentle, comforting man in his own house. Always.

My mother always had a temper. I saw it whenever her children were threatened. Never otherwise. Once, when I was suspended from school following a physical confrontation with a teacher, my mother lectured me about her dreams for me ... how I had to go to school, make something of myself, not act like a thug. Then she went to school for a conference with the principal and other officials, to discuss her son's future. During the conference, the teacher said I was a hoodlum. Only the timely intervention of several other officials saved him. From my mother.

Violence on the streets was not unknown to me. Violence inside the home seemed impossible.

My best friend was an abused child. I'd see the marks on him. He told me the truth. His father made no pretense otherwise. A weight lifter, inordinately proud of his physique, he often paraded around without a shirt so as to better display his accomplishments. I saw him brutally slap my friend for the sin of asking for catsup on his meat. I saw other things too. I never told my parents. You don't tell secrets. My best friend and I swore one day there would be revenge. When we were grown.

One day, my friend came to my house. His face was battered, blood on his mouth, running from his nose. He asked if he could hide in my basement — he was running away.

My father found us. Told my friend he could stay with us, but he would sleep in my room, not the basement.

His father came looking for him. My father met him in the front yard. We watched from the window.

My friend's father demanded that his son be produced. My father stood like a boulder, barring the way. My friend's father flexed his muscles. Words were exchanged. First about parental rights, then about children and what they needed.

Finally, my father asked the other man if he wanted to settle their dispute in the street.

The terrorist skulked away, muttering threats he never fulfilled.

We learn what we are taught. The greatest thrills of my life have come from the protection of children. My best friend later dropped out of school. Joined the army. When he returned, he settled with his father.

And never became a marine biologist.

I still miss him.

W

hat's going to happen?" she asked, holding my hand, looking up.

We were in an empty courtroom, escorted inside by a burly court officer who knew what I was up to.

The little girl was a beauty; dark, luminous eyes dominating her delicate face. She had been her mother's pride and joy. A brilliant student, joyous and happy, a prodigy at the piano.

Then the nightmares started. And the music stopped.

A wonderful therapist worked with the child. Carefully, gently. And uncovered the truth. The little girl had been sexually abused.

The perpetrator was held to answer for his crimes. And denied them all.

There was no medical evidence of his evil. Only the child's testimony could bring justice.

I took her into the courtroom to prepare her for the ordeal. To familiarize her with the trappings of The Law: the high bench where the judge would sit in his black robes, the counsel tables where the warring attorneys would lie in wait. And the witness chair from which she would testify.

Her therapist told me what was inside the child: Fear. Guilt. Shame. Horror.

"What does she want?" I asked.

"She wants it to stop. She wants to be safe."

The little girl's knuckles were white from her death-grip on my hand.

I had her sit in the witness chair. Explained how everyone would be listening to her, how important she was.

"Will he be here?"

I knew who "he" was. A predatory pedophile, hiding his foulness behind a bland sociopath's mask. He was entitled to be there. Our laws give terrorists the right to "confront" their victims in courtrooms.

"Yes, he'll be there. But he'll never hurt you again."

"What if he does?" A child's voice, the trust raped from her psyche.

"He won't come near you," I promised. "He won't even get out of his chair."

"Really?"

"Yes. And this man, it's his job to make sure."

The child's eyes turned to my friend, the court officer. He nodded reassuringly, his face stern. "He won't do anything," the officer told her, his voice hard and cold, one hand absently patting the butt of his pistol.

I went through the process for her. Slowly. Explaining what everyone would do, how they would do it. But something was missing. I talked with her, patient, reaching for that key that would set her free.

I felt her terror. I told her that when the perpetrator's attorney raised his voice or pounded on the counsel table (all of which I knew he would do at some point), it meant he was scared.

"Scared?" she asked, skeptical.

"Sure," I told her. "Bad people are always afraid of the truth. It's hard work to make up lies and try to stick to them. But the truth, that's easy. All you have to do is tell the truth."

"I told you the truth."

"I know you did. I believe you. And soon, everyone will believe you. Then it will all stop. Forever."

"You swear?"

"Yes."

"You swear you'll make me safe?" Wanting a display of that mystical, cosmic control of reality children believe adults possess.

I knelt next to her, her little face inches from mine. Knowing how the beast had abused her trust. Broken his promises as he tried to steal her soul. "Listen to me, now," I whispered. "You'll make yourself safe, child. The truth will shine out of you. It will shine on that man like a bright light. And he'll be afraid, then. Not you, him. That's what the truth does."

The trial started. I called the child as the first witness, knowing the anxiety in her, the pain of waiting. She took her seat, dressed like an angel. The court officer winked at her. A brother officer stood directly behind the accused. His attorney objected strenuously. The officer stepped back about six inches, reluctantly, snarling under his breath, continuing to hover. I touched the child's hand, whispered "He's scared already."

She told the truth. Sometimes she cried, sometimes she held her little face in her hands. But it all came out. The man's attorney questioned her vigorously. She saw his fear, felt her own flee.

I was inside her mind as she responded, trying to will strength into her answers. As close to praying as I get.

She left the witness stand. And the gloves came off. Courtroom combat over the body of a child. Nobody gambles for higher stakes. It should not be the gamble that it is.

More witnesses followed. Evidence. Arguments.

She wasn't there when the verdict came down.

Guilty.

His guilt. Her innocence.

I walked down the courthouse corridors to where she waited, secure in a guarded room. One of the defense attorneys passed me in the hall. Said "Nice job," and walked on. A professional, shrugging off this result, ready for the next one.

I was there when they told her. Social workers explaining, her mother trembling.

She came over to me. "No more?" she asked.

"No more," I told her.

She hugged me so tightly it must have hurt.

No other way to account for the tears in my eyes.

*M**aybelle is thirteen.*

A glorious, raven-haired child, delicately walking the tightrope between girl and woman. Eager to be grown and away, but unwilling to relinquish a safe, sweet childhood.

This morning, Maybelle is sulking. She is a determined, strong-willed young girl. A woman-child with her own sense of style, blending her outfits with deft precision. She loves mathematics and MTV. She makes her own jewelry. And she battles with her mother. Constantly.

Last night's argument, last week's dispute, last month's quarrel ... temporarily forgotten, and instantly capable of resurrection. Who knows what possesses the child today?

But her pout is prominent.

Maybelle comes to the table. Stands just behind her mother.

Addresses all her conversation to me.

Don't I think girls her age should be allowed to wear elaborate make-up?

No. I don't think girls her age should be allowed out of the house.

She giggles, dismissing it as banter.

If her mother said the same thing, it would precipitate an explosion.

They both know this.

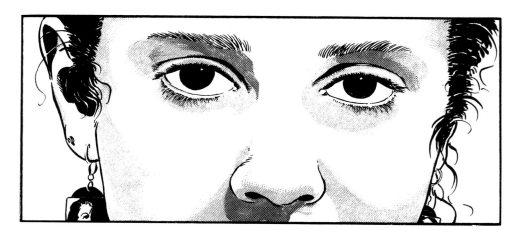

My mother is mean, the child says. Sometimes I really don't like her.

As she says this, her hands lose themselves in her mother's glossy mane. So much like her own. She pulls the long hair off her mother's neck, piles it on top of her head.

Wouldn't she look better if she wore her hair up? Wouldn't it be more stylish?

Talking to me with her lips — to her mother with her hands.

Your mother is lovely as she is.

But she dresses so ... old-fashioned, the girl replies.

I shrug my shoulders — nobody asks me for fashion advice.

Maybelle is still pouting, still arranging her mother's hair.

Oh, let's try it your way, her mother says, with just the trace of a soft smile.

In a minute, Maybelle is working furiously with hairpins and ribbons,

the pout banished before the concentration on her face.

She finishes.

Isn't she beautiful? she asks, displaying her work.

Mother and daughter never looked more alike.

*T*he apartment was a railroad flat, the rooms laid out end to end, one opening into another in a straight line. The front room was the parents' bedroom, the next would have been the living room, but the birth of two little girls turned it into a bedroom as well. The kitchen was against one wall of the girls' room, the bathroom outside, in the hall, to be shared with the other tenants.

The childrens' room was the nerve center: the outside door opened into that room, two windows provided sunlight, the fire escape welcome relief from the blistering summer heat.

Bedtime was sundown.

The mother tucked her children in, kissed them each, promised sweet dreams. Sometimes the father told them a story.

The two little girls were close in age, but very different. The older was introspective, quick-witted, determined to be a scientist when she grew up. The younger was a chubby extrovert, adventurous and bold. She wanted to be a police officer.

The father hated dogs — he'd been badly bitten by a stray when he was a child, and never had a dog of his own. But the little one had begged for a puppy — and the older one pointed out a whole stream of alleged advantages to possession of an animal. Each was certain that her own particular brand of advocacy had produced the result — Pepper, a fox terrier, rescued from the local pound.

Often, when their parents retired for the night, the little one would climb in bed with her older sister. And the older one would tell stories such as their father never dreamed. Tales of dragons and warriors, of mystical creatures and legendary feats. She was a born storyteller, and her little sister's appetite never waned.

One night, late, they heard an ugly scratching sound. The older girl didn't need a vivid imagination to tell her the source — rats, scurrying for food. Close by.

The younger girl, normally fearless, held her breath.

"Will they come after us?" she whispered.

Her sister held her finger to her lips, remembering tales of rats chewing on infants. Surely they were too old — it couldn't happen to them.

Pepper, the fox terrier, trembled. But not with fear. He was as rigid as a steel bar in the girls' bed, every nerve alert. Suddenly, he launched himself onto the floor, claws scraping for a purchase on the polished wood. A quick yip, then silence.

In the morning, there was no sign of the rats.

The children told their father, and he set massive traps, warning the girls never to go into the kitchen at night.

That night, he spent a long time with the girls, telling them they had nothing to fear.

"Pepper will protect us," the older child said, her hand on her sister's shoulder.

The father shared a look with the mother.

When the parents went to their bedroom, the older girl called for her dog. For the first time, Pepper refused to climb on the bed. No amount of coaxing could sway the little dog. He stationed himself against the far wall and lay down.

The rat-sounds woke the children. The back windows let in the faint reflected glow from the streetlights. The girls saw Pepper at his post, unmoving.

The rats made a high-pitched squeaking sound, smelling the cheese. It seemed like hours to the little girls, but the traps never sprung.

The older girl heard the rats worrying at the cheese. She trembled, despite the heat.

Suddenly, a dark shape flashed into the kitchen. Pepper. A sharp shriek, sounds of tiny claws. A distinct thump on the floor.

All was quiet.

Pepper trotted back inside, lightly leaped onto the bed. The girls slept against his small, warm body.

In the morning, the father found the rat on the kitchen floor, its neck broken. The cheese was gone from the traps.

For the first time, he called Pepper to him. "You're a hell of a dog," he told the fox terrier, his eyes on his children.

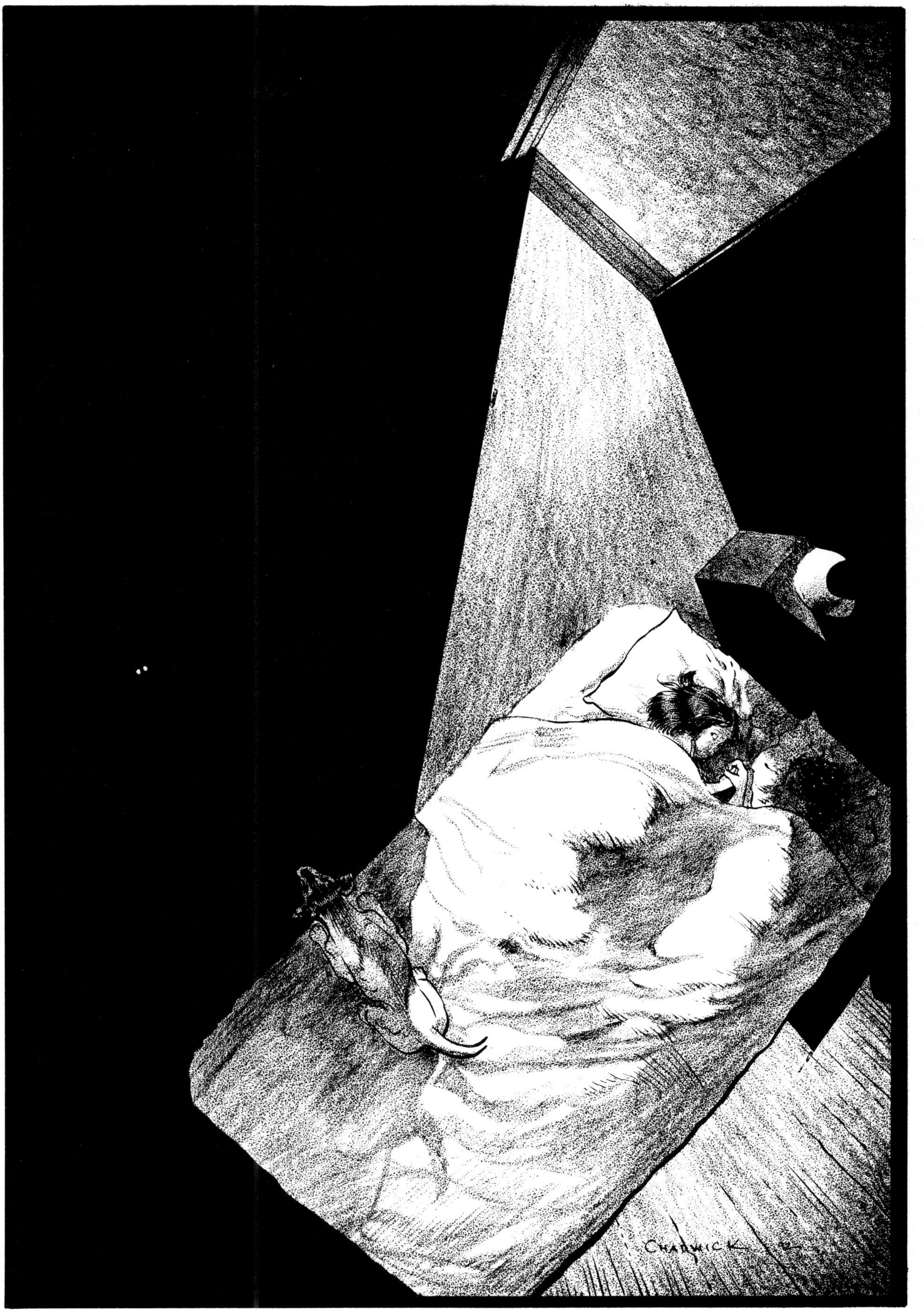
CHADWICK

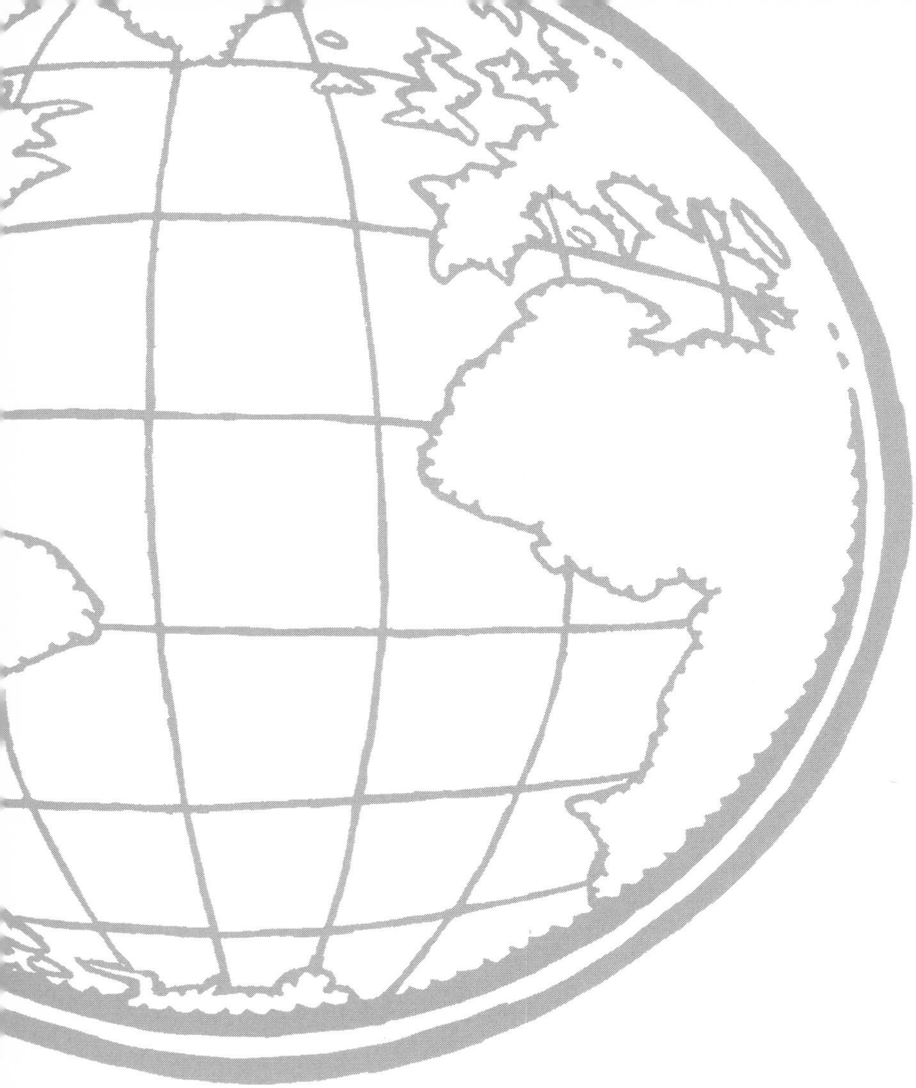

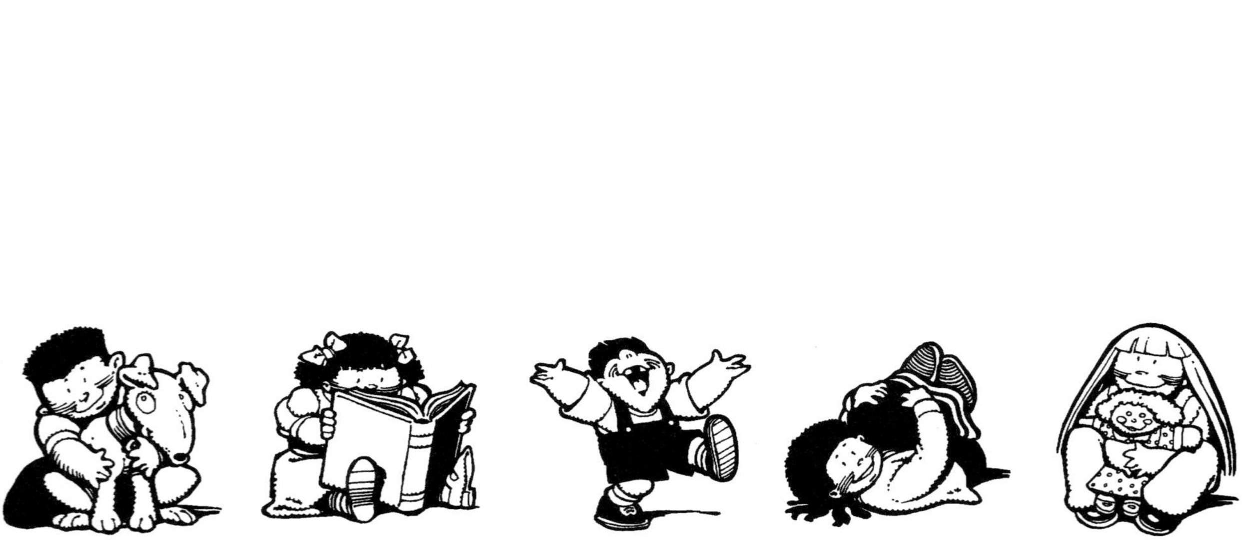

*C**hildren of the world.* Future flowers, now seeds. Some hand-raised, nourished in love-richened ground. Others tossed carelessly on the coldest concrete, struggling beneath Darwin's dispassionate sunlight.

Each unique, snowflake-individualized. And all the same.

Our race. The human race.

One color — many shades.

Treasures to some, toys to others.

They will reach the stars and stalk the shadows.

What children are, more than anything else, is this: another chance for our flawed species. Another chance to get it right.

***A**ndrew Vachss* has been a field investigator for the United States Public Health Service in Ohio, a social casework supervisor in New York City, and has directed programs for urban migrants in Chicago, a re-entry center for ex-convicts in Boston, and a maximum security prison for youth in Massachusetts. He has also worked as a community organizer, a criminal justice planner, a designer of institutions and programs, and for the relief effort in Biafra. Now an attorney, his private practice is exclusively devoted to representation of children and youth. Mr. Vachss is the author of *The Life-Style Violent Juvenile* and numerous articles and essays on the inextricably intertwined subjects of child abuse and juvenile violence as well as the Burke series of novels, including *Flood*, *Strega*, *Blue Belle*, *Hard Candy*, *Blossom*, and *Sacrifice*, which have been translated into more than a dozen languages.

ILLUSTRATION CREDITS

Tim Bradstreet
pages 52 - 56

Paul Chadwick
pages 7, 9, 19, 59

Geof Darrow
pages 26 - 43

Rick Geary
pages 4, 10, 11, 12, 16, 17, 22, 44, 45, 60, 61

Gary Gianni
pages 48 - 51

Dave Gibbons
pages 23 - 25

Warren Pleece
page 47

Paul Chadwick
cover illustration

Jerry Prosser & Randy Stradley
editors

Special thanks to:
Carolyn Scheuermann • book design
Mark Cox • cover design
Chris Chalenor • cover colors

Mike Richardson • publisher
Neil Hankerson • executive vice president
David Scroggy • vice president of publishing
Lou Bank • vice president of sales & marketing
Andy Karabatsos • vice president of finance

If you would like to order another copy
of this book, or if you would like to
have a copy sent to a friend, please call
1-800-862-0052 between 1:00 p.m.
and 4:00 p.m., PST.